Amateur Thoughts:

A Personal Collection of iWrite Poetry & LRW Quotes

Liltera R. Williams

Copyright © 2012 by Liltera R. Williams

iWrite4orU Publishing

PO Box 551006,

Jacksonville, FL 32255

(904) 566-2964

Website: www.iwrite4oru.com

Email: iwrite4oru@gmail.com

ISBN: 978-0-615-71054-9

Cover Designed by: Riana Winters

2

Write On!

(Noun): an exclamatory phrase that expresses excitement when good news is shared or received.

(Verb): an exclamatory phrase that encourages the action of expressing yourself.

Table of Contents

Acknowledgements
Introduction
Poems

- Amateur Thoughts: Discovered
- Skinny Girl, Fat Dreams
- Writer Itch
- Spell Check
- Ode to Self
- LoveHate (Pantoum)
- Forgotten
- I Confess
- Hungry War, Eating on Empty
- Because
- Lyrically Speaking
- Realistic Realization
- Without You
- Child of Complacency
- My Life
- I'm a Mess... Stressed
- Dreaming

- Fro Better or Fro Worse
- E-V-O-L LOVE
- Sideline Superman
- Whitman Imitation
- I'll Strive
- Confessions of a Writer
- Know This (Sestina)
- Let Me Go... No!
- Mathematic Love
- Reciprocated Truth
- What is Coincidence?
- Superwoman's Superman
- The End
- Reflections

iWrite Stanzas
LRW Quotes

"Lord knows dreams are hard to follow... but don't let anyone tear them away."

–Mariah Carey (Hero)

Acknowledgements

God is Great! We are all born with a gift and I was blessed to discover mine early. I shall thank HIM first and forever. Family is everything. Without the support of my loved ones, I would not be where I am today. Mom and Dad: Thank you for always guiding me, providing for me, and encouraging me to do what makes me happy. Thank you to my grandparents for sharing your wisdom and insight from various life experiences. Bro: I appreciate you for looking up to me and motivating me to become a prime example of a "Big Sister" success. To my aunts and uncles: Thank you ALL for being there as secondary protective guardians. To my cousins: Thank you ALL for being close confidants during my adolescent years. Friends are necessary. G.A.C for Life! Love is complicated. To the two men I once loved: Thank you both for offering me an opportunity to forgive and then move on to loving myself FIRST. Dreams are real. To my readers: Thank you for supporting my #WriterGrind. I am infinitely inspired. — LRW

Introduction:

Writing saved me, both literally and figuratively. Documenting my feelings and analyzing every single emotion allowed me to discover my true self. I was a girl who simply wanted to be loved. Now, I am a woman on a mission to spread love through language.

Express yourself by doing what you love and loving what you do...

#WriterGrind

POEMS

Amateur Thoughts: Discovered

I grew up in the hood where it wasn't all good
Free lunch at the community center
Summer was a tie with winter
They gave us free gifts when Christmas came
but Santa wasn't a fan of the ghetto games

Cornerball, Hide and Seek
Hopping over fences, Climbing trees
Jumping out of swings
Knocking on doors and running like thieves

While I was shooting basketballs
in hoops with no nets
my grandmother was hanging clothes outside
on the lines when they were wet
She yelled at us one by one
to come in before dark
Kicked the neighborhood kids off of her grass
and told them to go play at the park
She practically owned that hood
where it wasn't all good

and I was happy there once upon a time
Freedom was all mine because I stayed out of trouble
when others stayed in it
Didn't do anything until my homework was finished

13

They expected me to succeed
even though I didn't know how to lead
No one would listen to a goody two shoes
I was walking on thin ice
Doing everything they asked of me
Hoping I'd get it right

I could not fail
What kind of story would I tell
if I didn't stand out from the crowd?
I had to make mama and daddy proud
and my brother was looking up to me
when my cousins no longer wanted to be
stuck with me
I was not like them and they were ashamed
because I was strange
A natural born achiever
They begged for me to change
I guess I was an embarrassment
to their newfound fame

So many bad memories down that lane
I wanted to remain sane and free
Didn't want the police chasing after me
They caught so many criminals
on Emerson Street
that I was afraid to tell my address
when teachers asked me to speak

It wasn't even where I permanently resided
but I spent more time at grandma's
than I spent in silence
There was no such thing as private

Shared bath water with others
Slept close under the covers

It was no amazing grace...
I desperately longed for space from
Stray bullets, cocaine
Gold teeth and gold chains
That type of high life
would not become my life

They didn't understand my quest
I wanted to fly out of that nest
No option was better than the rest:
Keep it real or lose your life
Smoke a blunt or carry a knife
Learn to shoot guns for fun
When you see red and blue lights just run
Shoot dice and sell drugs for money
When they ask you who committed a crime
Act like a dummy
Snitchin' ain't cool
Drop out of school

Break all the rules
Steal from strangers
because working is for fools

What else can I say?
They already thought that I thought
I was better anyway
I just wanted to make it out of that hood
that wasn't all good
I wanted to be great

So I went off to Florida State
it was the perfect escape
and I got a small taste
of what the real world was like
It reminded me of those times
when I wished I was white
but I was happy to be the only colored girl
in most classes
a unique but sweet blackberry molasses
with no sense of fashion
Writing was my passion
That's all I knew
Words filled my notebooks and that passion grew
After I graduated
my **Amateur Thoughts** were anticipated
like breaking news
now I openly and willingly share them with you…

Skinny Girl, Fat Dreams

I didn't write today
Inspirational starvation
Took me a while to figure it out
Guess I forgot
Mental retardation

Mirrors block my vision
Only end goals in sight
Chewing on old emotions
Too hungry to see the light
I blink
Still not clear
Throwing up ideas, choking on my fears
It makes me sick

But I keep binging until I'm full
Can't take much more
Overloaded to the core of my existence
Try to resist it but I can't

So I'll continue to suffer

Feasting until death
'til there's no more of me left
as skin sheds from my bones
Heart beating alone
Anorexic mentality
Empty thoughts of success
Obese with desire
Faith beaming through my chest
Hiding ugly parts
Scars that show defeat
Can't let them witness the weaker side of me

So I cry alone
dreaming through tears

Piece by piece I stay together
The weight of the world won't break me

Writer Itch

I'm addicted to rhyming
My words must match
Can't reveal secret truths
without scribbling the facts
Take that, take that you irritating scratch!
Every time you bother me
new ideas begin to hatch
My creativity is struck like a match
and I burn you with my ability to hack
your complicated game of stones and jacks

I think I deserve a pat on the back,
maybe a trophy or even a patch
for getting rid of you
every time you maneuver through the cracks
Causing my eyes to turn red
and my mind to swell
Ohhh but if you were the sin
that could send me to hell
I'd still wish you well
I love your smell
and your aggravating touch

When you're not around I miss you THIS much
Keep making me blush
Never shut me up
Your presence is the reason for my
expressive hush
I just can't sweep away the floating dust,
the particles of this lovely lust
You're my necessary must

The lamp to my switch
The Abercrombie to my Fitch
The catcher of my pitch
and even when I throw a fit
You keep on caressing me with your itch
Let's get hitched
so you can bother me forever
Through freezing nights you'll be my sweater
and we'll keep warm together

I don't want to feel better
if it means losing the poems and letters
that I've produced from our endeavors
When I'd rather unwind, relax, and chill light,
you remind me to fight and force me to write

Even when I've lost my sight,
you're my guide through pain and strife
I know sometimes I ignore you
when you've reached your height
but I always scratch
and you always come back
I promise that I'll rub you for life

Spell Check

There's more to writing than organized words
While studying adjectives, nouns,
predicates and verbs
I've learned
how to manipulate the English language
in order to be heard
I'm superb
Known to irk nerves
by constantly correcting those who incorrectly infer
that *their* means *there* and *where* means *were*

Misplaced letters make a big difference
but illiterate misfits seem to forget this
and it pisses me off
In those oddly arranged sequences meanings are lost
and I pay the cost for righting your flaws
Careless errors
T's left uncrossed
Time is no factor
It takes just a second to pause
and execute the rules of grammar you were taught

Silly mistakes have brought this issue to my attention
Proofread your words out loud and listen
Add commas when they're missin'
A period to end that sentence

This problem is worth fixin'
So let's focus on nippin' it in the bud
because I'm exhausted and tired of
going above and beyond
editing lengthy run-ons,
incomplete thoughts that don't make sense,
improper past and present tense,
no capitalization or punctuation
A problematic situation
Unbelievable crisis we're facin'
If we continue misguidin'
the proper laws of writin'

If you're easily offended
and my rant gets you fired up
I'm not a fighter
but take this as a verbal tongue tied punch

Next time you're stuck
Down on your luck
Thinking way too much
About to give up
Take a breath
Count to two
Then ask yourself
What in the world would a writer do?

Ode to Self

I'm sorry for neglecting you
I've been very busy lately
Don't have enough time to create a rhyme
Even though there's a lot on my mind

Wish I had a better excuse
for not paying you much attention
but nothing justifies my actions
No matter how many explanations I mention

I just want to apologize
for ignoring your cries and calls
Lying to you and pretending like
I have nothing to say at all

Forgive me for denying my thoughts
Sometimes they're hard to understand
That's still no logical reason
for not curving a pen to my hand
Putting it to paper
and letting the words flow

Just ask me why I haven't been writing
I'll simply tell you I don't know
because that's the answer closest to the truth
So I won't waste my breath
Telling lies to you

Sorry

I'm apologizing one last time
for refusing to force myself to create a rhyme
That's truly a crime
but I'll pay the fine
and arrange my feelings
as I prepare to express
every single emotion
Get it all off my chest

I'll sit here until I'm finished
Even if it takes me all night
No matter how hectic things get
I promise you…

I'll write

LoveHate (Pantoum)

A thin line between love and hate
It stretches forever
There is no end
Just an infinite length of unidentifiable emotions
It stretches forever
Struggling to create a balance of security
Just an infinite length of unidentifiable emotions
Dwindling on a disordered route to happiness
Struggling to create a balance of security
Still strong enough to handle excess baggage
Dwindling on a disordered route to happiness
Where feelings linger, waiting to be clarified
Still strong enough to handle excess baggage
A thin line between love and hate
Where feelings linger, waiting to be clarified
There is no end

Forgotten

24 hours in a day and I can't even
get a second of your time
Am I not worth a minute or two?
Reserved durations for nonstop communication
Just me and you?

Instead it's
Drive-by moments and casual nights of love molding
I'm beginning to wonder if you're thinking of her
when it's me that you're holding

If I'm not worthy of your ticks and tocks
Then return the key to my heart's lock
and let me breathe again
I tried to be your trusted friend
but you refused to let me in

Whether filled or spare, my time was never bare
Though you were rarely there
Just a figment of your flesh
as you pleased me less and less

I didn't ask to be invited into your mess
Still I resided in your troubled nest
and watched you fight the battle of being depressed

Now I'm picking up the pieces
of the pain you left me with
While someone else is enjoying
love's sweet privileges

I guess my loyalty and commitment to us
just wasn't enough
You wanted more than I was willing to give up
Yet all I wanted was an ounce
of what you hold inside
The opportunity for us to climb and become more
than what I dreamed I'd find

I wish you could say the same
if the tables were twisted
Told you if I had to choose I'd risk everything
that I have to lose
and you dismissed it
You murdered our love and stripped it

Now I can't fast forward the digits

So I rewind to the memories of your wrongs
and every time I feel the urge to pause
reminisce and prolong
I'll remember exactly why I decided to move on

Forgetting you will be hard at first
but someday I'll get over this hurt
and realize how much I'm really worth

I'll no longer have to beg for your time
While your days are full of loneliness
There will be happiness in mine
and you'll regret the day you let me fly

I'll spread my wings as they become tall
smile as I recall the times you let me fall
and a new face will take your place
as the seconds, minutes, and hours pass away

I Confess

I'm not the person I used to be
The world has gotten the best of me
I thought that I had been set free
but my eyes were closed and I couldn't see
blinded by my insecurity
Wishing to be someone else
Losing love for myself
Lower than I've ever felt
I tried to be perfect but it didn't work
because in the end I still got hurt

Nowhere to turn in times of need
Crying as my soul would bleed
Willing to follow anyone's lead

I learned to love but it wasn't enough
to fill the void
so I'm giving it up

All by myself that's how it's always been
Just me alone drowning in my sins
Asking for forgiveness over and over again

I'm sorry to disappoint you
I don't mean to fail
but lately I haven't been doing too well
I've forgotten what's important in life
Embracing the wrong and ignoring the right
My heart is too weak to put up a fight
So I go for the ride and hold on tight

Waiting to fall because I always do
Then get up and come running right back to you
and you never reject me, no matter what I've done
It's just a shame that you're the only one

There have been so many days that I wanted to quit
Counting every step wondering how far I'd get
I've survived this long without trying my best
and from this day forth I will give you no less
as I make an effort to clean up this mess
I'll continue to press without any rest to pass your test

I confess

Amen

Hungry War, Eating on Empty

I'm
having a hard time
trying
to fully digest this feeling

You're full of shit
and I can't commit
to any man who's willing to treat me
the way you didn't

You screwed me
Misused me and abused me
Impregnated me with lies
and left me to push on my own
Alone
with no apology for doing me wrong
Now I'm struggling to move on

I hate that I love you
Love that I hate you
Still I can't erase you
and it hurts

You treated me like dirt
When I put you first
So if nice guys finish last
Then why am I the one who can't get past
the pain

Going insane
Trying to regain my dignity
Look at what you did to me!
We were never meant to be
Now I know, but I can't let go
and it's killing me

I'll never understand
why you couldn't be the man I needed
You cheated and left me defeated
Wish I would have seen it
I knew you didn't mean it
when you said you loved me
Would put no one above me
Damn you for taking advantage of me
But I'll be OK

Soon I'll find my way
and you'll be the one hoping for the day
you can have me back
but then it will be too late

The first step was clearing you from my plate

Still I'm
having a hard time
trying
to fully digest this feeling

My heart tries to remind me
of my worth
but there's nothing here that can quench
my thirst
So I burp right before I burst
and then I realize
No matter how much it hurts
There's always room for dessert

Because...

Its vernacular isn't defined by a particular language
Letters weld together to create enticing words,
the reflection of thoughts on paper
Punctuation isn't necessary, but optional
It's the most therapeutic form of expression
There is no wrong way to write it
If it didn't exist, music would be a lonely melody
without lyrics
The rules of English don't apply
to the fabricated vocabulary you choose to construct
It's an elaboration of the imagination,
the art of eloquence
Documented feelings dance
to the beat of composition
and oral execution edifies each line

Poetry is the air that breathes life into the world

Lyrically Speaking

Music is my soul,
the method of my existence
A day without song leaves me drifting
in the distance

I function to the beat
It guides me as I jive
Can't eat, can't sleep,
can't think, can't drive
without the fuel that keeps me alive

The rhythm gets me moving
Left, right, forward
Constant inspiration
for the goal I'm leaning toward

One listen to a tune
Now my day can begin
The hours tick by and the same way
it ends

Words ignite in me
a pyrrhic sensation

So I write
until I reach an emotional revelation

Harmonious sounds caress my ears
and release me from all of my constricting fears

I'm free…

Not a victim of soundless tranquility
but an obsessor of beautiful melody
I can see, I can breathe,
I can dream, I can be

Because I have Music and Music has me

Realistic Realization

I have manipulated myself into believing
that intelligence resides within me
Ignorant to common practices,
Yet knowledgeable about content
that is unfamiliar to my communal comrades

I struggle with a conflict between
street and book analogies
Wanting to forget the negative aspects
of my environmental surroundings
Unable to retain the new ideas that attack me daily

Because I am obligated to be loyal
to the background of my being,
I must always remember the foundation
that molded my character

Still, I deserve the chance to reach
for unbreakable boundaries
and the opportunity to explore my limits

But I am confined by failure

Encompassed by individuals
who are afraid of success
rubbing off on me,
causing me to become hesitant in my quest
for a better life

Fortunately, I have been able to accept
my irreversible past,
conquer my inescapable present,
and tear down the walls of an impossible future

Intelligence is just an ideological theory and since my
ideas are theoretically correct, I guess I am
intelligently immune to those common practices that
seem to add to my everyday struggle of attaining the
desires that are fighting to be released from the
shackles of dreaming.

Without You

Without you I am free
Without you I am strong
Used to think that with you I belonged
Without you I can breathe
Without you I can see
Used to think that without you there was no me
Without you I can smile
Without you I can feel
Used to swear that without you I wouldn't heal
Without you I can sleep
Without you I won't cry
Used to believe that without you I would die
Without you I am better
Without you I am good
Without you I can do all the things
I never thought I could
Without you I can move on
Without you I can forgive
Without you I can be
Without you I can live

Child of Complacency

You refuse to explore new ideas and conceptions
Reluctant to change
Content with familiar things
Comfortable in your misery
Unable to make me happy
because you are too afraid of difference

Yet, you expect me to wallow with you
To swim in your royal river of regret
While you remain stuck in the past,
holding on to hardship,
elongating the pain

Why do you run from manly duties?

You must find pleasure in your childish ways
Though it's not healthy
to expand childhood
It is meant to exist as an era of the past
Much like us
Not destined to last

Your ego is stroked by immature acts
Satisfaction comes from your masterful trickery,
scheming to keep my affection
taking advantage of my passion
and desire for love
in order to soothe your fear of loneliness

I have grown tired of your stale commitment
Finally ready to escape this unworthy situation
So I'm crawling away from this handicapped affair
until I am able to walk alone

My Life

It may seem as if I have it all together
but my feelings flip as quickly as a feather
Mom, there are some things you don't know about me
and dad, I'm not the teen that you thought I would be
My eyes have been so blind these past few years
I've prayed numerous times and shed many tears
I'm all grown up now, time to do things on my own
but please don't allow me to face this experience alone
I feel like there is no one on whom I can depend
and away goes the fun whenever I lose an old friend
I try to be independent by doing responsible things
but my pain is extended from all the stress that brings
I'm not complaining,
although I've had some tough times
separating phony foes from true friends of mine
The story of my life is a good one to tell
because things wrong gone right turned out so well

I'm A Mess... Stressed

School, work, family, and friends
No matter what I do I can't seem to win

Grades in school aren't what they should be
Too tired to study because things are bothering me
Work is tough
but I need a job to keep me on my feet
Still don't have enough money
So it's hard to make ends meet

Family doesn't miss me
No one picks up the phone to call
I'm starting to believe that they don't love me at all

Fighting to keep my relationship
from coming to an end
Struggling, trying to make time for my friends
It doesn't matter which way I bend
because even at my best I feel like less

I'm a mess... Stressed

Dreaming

I exist to you, but to them I'm a ghost
Floating through the world invisible to most
Am I here? Am I there?
This can't be real
The flesh of my bones I cannot feel
I'm asleep
Thoughts are dead
Nothing but dreams filling up my head

My future is clear when my eyes are closed
I'm able to see the direction in which my life goes
Just stuck in a dream, somewhere in between
a fairytale and reality, or so it seems

I can't escape so I lie there and wait
for someone to rescue me from my dormant state
but I'm afraid that it may be too late
because I don't want to wake up
and have to start anew
or face the fact that my dreams may not come true

So I sleep

Fro Better or Fro Worse

Fro is mini
Thoughts are plenty
Didn't go natural because it's trendy

Understand who I am behind this hair
Doesn't matter if it's barely there
I'm aware of how people talk and what they've said
Rumors that they firmly embed
Regurgitating the lies they're fed
Such a shame how quickly it spreads
Infecting innocent ignorants who believe
that those with dreads
represent a gang of thuggish criminals
trying to prove their street cred

Silly misguided special eds!

These pilus threads growing out of my head
have led me to a place of security
a confident surety
That helped me to see the redefined pure in me

Tired of explaining to those who lack the will
to comprehend
that this is more about where I'm going
and less about where I've been
Went back to my roots but that wasn't the main cause
I'm on a mission to embrace my hidden flaws
In relaxers and weaves
My self got lost and I paid the cost

I shouldn't have to be a different me for show
Must I wrap myself up in a big red bow?
Prettify this skin, a faded color of crow
and conform to what others claim to know?
Underneath the naps and kinks
is way more than what you think
I'm unique, distinctly distinct
and on the brink of a breakthrough
That you'll miss if you blink

I see myself in a mirror that glows
deep reflections of a renewed soul
So respect my struggle
and acknowledge my growth
the next time you judge me by my fro!

E-V-O-L LOVE

I'm done with trying to figure out what it means
I decided finally to just
let it be
You see
The more you think about it
the harder it is to understand it
and the more you crave it
the more your heart demands it

but you can't force it
It has to happen naturally
because that's the only way to explore its pure beauty

I get it now
and it's a remarkable revelation
but confusion comes with it
and then
there's frustration
Not knowing how to hold on to something
worth preserving
and not knowing whether to give it to someone
who's deserving

In life you must take chances
The same goes for this too
You can't be afraid to explore something new

Most people spend their whole lives not knowing
what it means
defining it by things that they envision
in their dreams
but it's not something you can just make up
It's an emotion that you feel
and those living in fear of realizing that
are the ones who don't believe it's real
Still

L-O-V-E
It sucks!

It takes up all of my time
and makes me think too much
I still can't understand it
no matter how hard I try
and I don't get how it makes me smile
but at the same time cry

I was so sure it was in me
to L-O-V-E you completely
but now I'm having second thoughts
because of all the pain it has brought
my way
I'm always feeling sad and constantly having
bad days

This isn't L-O-V-E
It just can't be
because there's no way that LOVE
would do this to me
So I'm sorry for making you believe
something that really wasn't

A lot of things make me happy but
L-O-V-E doesn't

Sideline Superman

The armor wearing knight, pick-me-up type
when your man ain't doin' right
Every woman needs a Sideline Superman in her life

He's waiting patiently to enter the game
but she keeps wanting more of the same
pain and disappointment
A recurring cycle of abuse
All he wants is a chance to reverse the hurt
and show her what a real man is supposed to do

Good guys finish last because good girls
continue to pass on all they have to give
We'd rather waste time on the fine guy
who approached us first dibs
instead of allowing Clark Kent
to use his superpower gifts
A sad story that usually ends with broken hearts
The bad guy crushed her to pieces
while Sideline Superman was sitting on the bench
picking up the parts

He would have never made her cry
but when she finally builds up the strength
to say goodbye to the bad guy
Sideline Superman is no longer wearing his disguise
She couldn't get to him in time
A bad woman had already become his kryptonite

The game continues and they end up as friends
but neither one can find the strength
to repeat where they've been
If only she would have given him a chance
from the start
instead of letting those villains
permanently damage her heart

The fear of being alone came back to haunt her again
but she's still holding on to the love she has within

Next time she'll know how to handle it right
and if she happens to find another
armor wearing knight pick-me-up type
she'll jump at the chance to let him make her his wife
because every Superwoman deserves
to have a Superman in her life

Whitman Imitation – Song of Myself: Section 50

There is something in you — I think I know what it
is — and I know it is in you. Covered and cold —
still and silent then you become, I pause — I pause
long. I do not know it — it is without name — it is a
secret well kept, it is not easily seen, felt, heard.
Something it shines through more than a radiant
light. To it the reflection is the image whose face
reveals you. Perhaps there could be more.
Descriptions! I pray for my friends and enemies.
Do you see O my friends and enemies? It is not
hatred or animosity — it is emotional, passionate,
deep — it is eternal life — it is love.

I'll Strive

Looking back on things I've done
I feel somewhat ashamed
It's hard to make good out of
the things that caused me pain

Feeling so alone thinking no one really cared
but longing just for someone
who would always be there
Remembering the past
is a difficult thing to do
especially when everyone
has found ways to hurt you

True happiness is rare
It's a once in a lifetime thing
but when it is present
forever joy is what it brings

I'll just keep waiting for the future to arrive
leaving all the pain behind me
walking blindly
I'll strive

Confessions of a Writer

They say writers are crazy
creatively insane
got complicated issues clouding our brains
treating words like drugs
addicted to the high of depicting details
as time flies by

Letting ink flood pages
a linguistic shower
cleansing to our souls
so we indulge in it for hours

Syllabic organization
cooperating rhymes
working hard to situate ideas
taking over our minds

We set the standard for language
create idioms that you speak
allowed slang to become accepted vernacular
for practices that you preach

Authors, journalists, critics, writers all the same
teammates playing together in this composition game

They told me I wouldn't succeed
if I relied on such a craft
and every time they said it
I let out a dismissing laugh
because the world of writing is endless
there is no right or wrong path

My vocabulary is self-made
I create my own words
read dictionaries for leisure
guess I'm an educated nerd

Don't knock my occupation
I won't go down without a fight
when people ask what I do for a living
I cringe with all my might
because to me it's not a job
It is a way of life

In words I find peace,
taken to unbelievable heights

floating between days and nights
composing scenes in dark and light
releasing emotions
that reside deep inside,
sometimes packed too tight

Once let out they shine so bright
emitting a powerful force, firmly granite
causing a creation of beautiful, concrete images
intriguing to my sight
whether black and white or colored stripes

iWrite
in spite
of what I see

Know This (Sestina)

Ignorance is a blissful failure of the mind
One who succumbs to simply not knowing
chooses to be defeated by the wrath of stupidity
Knowledge is a powerful tool of destruction
and only those who attain its prevalence
will overcome life's trying obstacles

It is logical to be intimidated by obstacles
Don't let false entities overtake your mind
because those who avoid fear prevail
Create an advantage by using what you know
Allow your intelligence to cause mass destruction
While others wallow in their stupidity

Laugh at those who dare to call you stupid
For they are merely the smallest obstacle
standing in the way of the destruction
birthed from the depths of your mind
The amount of damage thereafter is unknown
But in success you will surely prevail

It is your destiny to reach pure prevalence
and escape the hidden traps of stupidity
already understanding the outcome, knowing
that you can't be defeated by tough obstacles
So sit back and arrange the visions of your mind
Let your brain flow with thoughts of destruction

Remember not to boast over what you destruct
You will regretfully reverse your prevalence
and lose control over your mindfulness
eventually leading yourself into stupidity
Tripping over disguised, invisible obstacles
Unable to take advantage of what you know

Illiteracy is an evil ally to the unknown
Being blind to words ultimately leads to destruction
especially when knowledge is shielded by obstacles
and there are limited accounts of those who prevail
due to an inability to separate ignorance & stupidity
Becoming dumb, losing control of their minds

A smart mind knows and recognizes signs
that appear before letting stupidity
lead it to destruction

Let Me Go... ~~No~~!

You're giving me reasons to tell you goodbye
but you won't let me leave
Keeping me trapped
Unable to adapt
It's hard for me to breathe

Why are you holding on
if you don't want me anymore?
I really don't understand
If the tables were turned I would let it burn
So please run while you can

I won't promise you forever
because the future can't be predicted
and waiting for time to just pass by
can leave you confused and afflicted

Love hurts sometimes but right now it's out to kill
So I'm saving myself before it's too late
and ignoring the way I feel
about you, about us
about commitment, about trust

Relationships never seem to turn out
the way you plan
No matter how hard we try
we will eventually disband

Why not save ourselves the heartache
and just end things now?
Moving on won't be easy
but we'll find a way somehow
I may not be wise but I'm smart enough to know
that this isn't going to work so just let me go...

No!

I love you so much it hurts
With each tear comes a new scar
Can't go back to the way we were
so I'm settling for what we are

It may seem strange to others
that I choose to live in pain
but I've forced myself to realize
with every loss there's a new gain

I'm teaching myself a lesson,
it's never too late to learn
Lovers often struggle,
I guess right now it's our turn

It makes no sense to end it here
when we've made it this far along
Holding on when times get rough
is what makes our love so strong

I'm not giving up on what we've built
so forget what I said before
I was speaking out of anger and frustration
I'm not ready to close the door
Not now, not ever
No matter how hard things get
Please hold on to me tight
Don't you dare say goodbye yet

I may not be wise
but I'm smart enough to know
That we belong together
So don't let me go

Mathematic Love

Love is evil
Goes around manipulating hearts
Forcing us to believe in the false image that it portrays
A lot like math
You must know the formula to solve the problems
That it creates
First you add a partner,
Subtract differences, and become one
Equals
At least until you reach that decimal point
When anger is multiplied
and you're struggling to find
the least common denominator
Digging deep down into the square root
Trying to reconnect
but the remainder is a reminder that you two
no longer fit together
Time is the greatest common factor
and you've been divided because of it
Numeral quantities
Disrupted by incorrect calculations
Just an incomplete equation with no solution

Reciprocated Truth

A lonely casualty devoted to love
but love doesn't love me
Nor does it comply with my heart

A struggle of emotional complexities
Leaves bloody feelings murdered by rejection

Endless possibilities lingering in the distance
Too far to grasp, but I reach anyway
Comforted by hope
Waiting to be rescued
from these suffocating thoughts

Dreams of forever became nightmares of goodbye
when incompatibility made itself known

You can't ignore what's right in from of you
but I look with blind eyes
Creating my own visions of a better reality
Still holding on to my ability to love
even if no one cares enough to love me back

What is Coincidence?

Not the accidental meeting you'd excuse with an
apology, an empty expression as if mark of a plan you
stretched your mind too far to, hoping for a way in,
nor the firmness in the "hello" you uttered, smiling
with a sneaky glare in your eye. Not the front you put
on, pretending like this is the first time you've see her
face. Not the possibility of being in the same place at
the same time as your virtual lover. Not the false
feelings that have enraptured your being, placing you
in an improbable state, so gone from reality. Not the
occurrence you constructed to put a hold on time, for
the official moment — an erroneous and deceptive
circumstance — beginning already, the plan
progressing. Not the speech with no error, her
reaction, empty as vacancy. Only the coldness of her
shoulder — tilted angle, pointed blade — her rudeness
growing with each second, the way all strangers' do.

Superwoman's Superman

He adores me like no one ever has before
My insecurities fall victim to his compliments
Crushed particles face down on the floor

Opposites attract but we match
His kisses make me melt
Third degree burning desires
from sparks I've never felt

I love the way he looks at me
with eyes that pierce straight through
Slight glare,
steady stare
I look back and see the truth

A generous gentleman who never forgets
to say please
and thank you
He'll make you wish for a guy with his traits
but only lucky girls score his kind
I was ready when he threw the bait

He needs me like I need him
Open my heart
I'll bleed him
Give me nine lives
I'll freeze them
to savor each moment I breathed him

A love like this doesn't happen every day
I'll surrender my powers
Give them up if I may
become one with my Superman
and fly far far away

The End

their love shatters to pieces
a fragment of hope
clouds the atmosphere
lovers have reverted to loneliness
inside wounded hearts
passion dwells
and it never sees the light
this is falsified fear
someone screams
disabling your desires

Reflections

I fell in love with writing at age 12
and married it at 18
I was always encouraged to follow my dreams
So I continue to expose what's deep beneath me
Started my own company at age 24
and at age 25 I was pushing for more
By 30 I'll be worthy of bestselling author praise
At 50, I'll be reflecting on my "old school" days
If I make it to 60, I'll still be spiffy
with my pen and pad with me
Writing out my life mysteries
and reminiscing about how I made history

Yeah, I'll make a difference alright
Even when I experience
discouraging days and nights,
I'll hold on to the range of change that I plan to ignite
and if someone decides to award me
for my improve the world fight
I'll gladly accept the honor and step in front of the mic

Tell my readers thank you
for following me on this flight
Spread my wings, soar to unbelievable heights
and continue to share my words
of encouraging might

When my life is finally over
I want others to be able to say
"She did all that she could
to make this space a better place"

If my papers should ever ruffle
or my tools run out of ink,
my stories will refuse to sink,
remaining firmly and eternally linked
to those who took the time to read and understand
my metaphoric kinks

I wear the title of writer proudly,
it's more than just a name
I'm a dignified dame
Leaving a trace as a leader of grace
The creative chick who uses language
to put a smile on someone's face

At 87 I'll still be writing my way to Heaven
and when I finally make it through those gates
I'll reminisce on the year 1986
The 23rd day of the eleventh month
and carve my name on the golden fronts
as a symbol of the gift that I was given
once upon a time
and when the sun shines
to the left of the light you'll find

"iWrite"

I moved on from the past that I left my mess in
to make room for an unlimited amount of blessins
and asked God to let me use my words as weapons
so if mirrors are connections
related to untainted inspections
my poetry collection will birth a legacy of affection
and every strategically constructed lesson
that I learned from my confessions
will allow me to be remembered forever
through my reflections

*i*WRITE STANZAS

*He's the man of my reality
 Dreams are overrated
 They say true love is hard to find
 What an overstatement

*Ideas clouding up my head
 need an umbrella for this pour
 rumbles of thunder, lightning galore
 run for cover, hit the floor
 There's a penning flood in store

*Time waits for no man
 It surely doesn't wait for me
 Afraid of who I'll become tomorrow
 but yesterday is who I used to be
 Looking back on my past
 Clear mind, closed eyes
 Memories of empty hellos
 and tick tocking goodbyes

*On my grind
Could care less about skinned knees
Picking at scabs
peeling and revealing my dreams
God told me to hold on
so I'm squeezing for dear life
"Don't give up," He said
"Everything will be alright"
allergic to patience
trying to pass the time
waiting for this miraculous cure
to ease my mind
My future is on the line
I'm scratching at the surface
of a goal that's all mine
successful aspirations, hindering binds
I'll be fine. Yes, I'll be fine.

*He loves me
He loves poetry
an epic form of adultery
like metaphors and similes
an intertwining symmetry
when he leaves my heart can't breathe
feels like we're playing make believe
I love me
I love poetry
but I love him three
because he loves poetry and he loves me

---

*He reads with me, prays with me,
wraps me in his arms
when he lays with me
He kisses me, misses me,
apologizes when he pisses me off
He even listens to me pointlessly talk
He walks the walk

---

*Sticks and stones may break my bones
but words will never hurt me isn't always true
The effects of verbal abuse last much longer
than physical wounds do
I'm a writer and you're using my biggest weapon
to cut me in two
but I'm halfway defensive
and halfway feeling sorry for you

---

*iWrite
Absorb me
or choose to abhor me
See, haters hate her
but she still makes her
hard-earned paper
Won't let them take her
Glory
I speak metaphorically
the truth rhetorically
words birthed from the core of me
uRead and want more of me
Addicted to what's stored in me
Begging for encores from me
Pause, play, stop, repeat
You're bringing out the roar in me

---

*I need a healing
Not the pill popping medicinal kind
but a still stopping freeing of the mind
Thoughts aren't aligned
Overlooking the things I'm hoping to find
How could I be so blind?
The heart wants what the heart wants
and I've always listened to mine
I'm at the line, about to decline
wondering if I should ignore it this time

---

*I saw it coming, but I closed my eyes
You can't hurt me if I don't oblige
I'm immune to love's allies
Won't give up now
Can't accept defeat
Even when they're weak
fragile hearts still beat

---

*I'm beautifully written
a chart-topping hit song
No one hit wonder
my catalog's long
Words make me pretty
like make-up tools
I break trend laws
and set my own rules
Uniquely different
selfishly vain
perfectly imperfect
creatively insane
and I won't change
If you can love me through the happy,
you can love me through the pain
learn my heart like you learned my name

---

*Lyrical lover is he, lyrical lovers are we
"I do" to his verse, for better or worse
'Til death do us part, I cross my whole heart
Through sickness and health,
poverty and wealth
I'll dedicate myself
All that I am
all that I'll be
forever and ever after
eternally

---

*As far as I can tell my parents taught me well
Trouble all around me
Lost souls living in hell
Burnt dreams, it seems they like the smell
I watched them dwell but I never fell
Drew the line, Clocked the time
Automatically saved by the bell

---

*Made it to 24, but I want more
More success and way less stress
I guess I'm ready for what's in store
If we remain unchanged at each age stage
then what do we need birthdays for?
I'm growing while knowing
that God is the reason I'm alive
Praying that I'll live to see
a better me at 25

*Irreconcilable differences
 Patching up my stitches with
 leftover pain and remnants
 No longer breaking dishes
 Instead I'm making wishes
 and if I could forget this love
 so trite and vicious
 Maybe I'd realize
 I'm worth a lot more

---

*Been sittin' on top of the world
 since I was a little girl
 No diamonds and pearls
 I had a Basketball Jones for midair curls
 and Jumpman Jordan twirls
 Swish!

---

*I want that can't get that old thing back
 because it never left
 hardly ever spend nights by myself
 kind of love

---

*What is a mother?

A prime example is all you've been to me
A combination of all that I pretend to be
Brave when trouble comes,
Strong when pain strikes
A beautiful Black woman who isn't afraid to fight
Someone who would go against every legal creed
to make sure that her children
have everything they need
She'll even sacrifice her own dream
Because great mothers understand
there's no "I" in team
My mother never complains about anything
I can't wait to see her smile
at the sight of her first grandchild
but for now she's OK with settling
for my fictional stunt
Unless, of course my brother beats me to the punch

*I'll write the pain away
 Erase you from my mind's recollections
 Ignore the beating of my heart's depression
 Take notes and digest this repetitive lesson
 Accept the facts
 and stop hypothetically guessin'
 When the ink runs dry
 at the end of goodbye
 I'll start a new chapter
 No more you and I

---

*No more ride or die
 My new focus is write or die
 Can't keep wrestling around on the ground
 with love
 when I'm trying to fly
 I'm so close to touching the sky
 I just might overdose on this natural high

---

*The path to success should not be traveled alone
 Wish I had someone there waiting for me at home
 My #WriterGrind can only give me so much
 I'm not always satisfied by my laptop's touch

---

*Today turns into tomorrow
 during my midnight sessions
 Writing what's on my mind
 as an attempt to pass the time
 and teach myself a new lesson

*You can reach for success with your hands
 but if your heart isn't attached
 to the plan
 You'll just end up walking
 on dry land
 and dehydration creates hesitation
 when dedication
 isn't enhanced
 I'd rather die trying
 instead of wishing
 that I was flying
 with those who dismissed
 the sight of fear
 at first glance
 I won't let being afraid to dance
 cause me to
 miss out on
 my big chance

*I miss you
 but it hurts that you don't miss me too
 Memories down the drain
 Hard to ignore this pain
 I'd take you back with my last heartbeat dance
 If only you were willing to give us another chance
 How could you forget all that we were to each other?
 Promises of forever
 Overshadowed by an unwanted goodbye
 Am I not worthy of one last try?
 I fought hard for you
 2 years and 12 rounds of the devil's abuse
 God was supposed to see us through
 but you stopped believing
 in what I thought we both knew
 I miss you
 and it hurts that you don't miss me too

---

*Words give me power
 Don't test me
 My ammunition is hefty
 I'll cut you with a noun in a minute
 and then shoot you down
 with a proper sentence

---

*Just when I get comfortable being by myself
 He comes back trying to steal my heart
 Intentional grand theft
 but this time I was strong enough to step
 To the left, to the left
 Left, right, left

*That dream I dreamed
 right before I turned 13
 is now a realistic scene
 of all the things I imagined
 success would bring

*Teary-eyed, brokenhearted
 Tried to get back to the way it was
 when we started loving each other blissfully
 but you were too busy for me
 Still I loved you unconditionally

*The pain from a broken heart is the worst
 form of distress on the road to success
 but unexpected quirks inspire hard work
 and there's no hurt where happiness lurks

*Hard work pays off and with every "eye" that I dot
 and negativiTy I cross
 They'll see how much I'm willing to fight
 without pause
 My #WriterGrind is more than just a dream
 It's an accumulation of my determination
 from all the failure I've seen
 I don't care much for shiny, expensive,
 limited edition things
 To reach the epitome of the gift that was given to me
 Is worth more than any type of gold
 or tarnished bling
 I'm on a mission that's beyond extreme
 and years from now
 they'll know exactly what I mean

---

*There's always room for improving yourself
 Success isn't measured
 by the attainment of wealth
 It's the desire to require the best
 from your flesh
 For blessings come to those
 who don't settle for less

---

*I just want to share my words
 with the world
 and prove that dreams can become realities
 if you ignore the technicalities
 and have faith
 Keep trying until you've reached
 the end of the race
 If no one else is willing to run with you
 Just set your own pace

---

*That moment when my eyes start getting heavy
 and I look at the clock and realize
 it's not even midnight yet
 I fight the temptation of procrastination,
 ignore the sleepy sensation
 and push through another hour
 to finish my latest writing creation

---

*I can't be a leader without faithful readers
 My words will lie dormant
 without loyal informants
 Please honor my hustle, respect my time,
 and kindly support my #WriterGrind

---

*Even if I'm not able to retire before age 68
and write for the rest of my days
while relaxing in my own space
as I count the wrinkles on my face
I'll find peace in knowing that I made it
to the finish line of my daily race
and conquered every single dream that I chased

---

*Selfless people know how to let go
Selfish people know how to say no
Helpless people know how to do both

---

*Those who care enough
to correct a significant mistake
before it's too late
will ultimately escape
a solitary life of regretful fate

---

*Some days I just want to wake up
and forget that you existed
The way you used to hold me tight
and promise that everything would be alright
I miss it

---

*I get high on my writer supply
 the only drug I need
 puff puff passing away at my dreams

---

*This dream I birthed was painful at first
 No matter how passionate you are
 failure still hurts
 What are the odds that my first two lovers
 Would break my heart
 and charge me with the same curse
 I never truly got over the first
 so I guess that's why
 the second time around it hurts even worse

---

*If distance makes the heart grow fonder
 Why does letting go
 make the pain last longer?
 I wonder
 If I'd never met you
 would my heart be stronger
 or would I still be starving
 from the constant hunger
 of wanting to be loved

---

*Hypothetically speakin
 I'm poetically leakin
 These aesthetically pleasing
 Verses have reason
 Love cuts have deepened
 and I can't stop the bleedin'

---

*Pen-Ultimate Glory

 iWrite to shed light on a mighty dim world
 Spending nights out of sight staring at my slim pearl
 As it glides across the pages, I watch the letters twirl
 and smile because I know they love to dance
 and my heart loves to sing
 The joy that writing brings can never be measured
 my words will forever be treasured
 like diamond rings

---

*Already famous
 Don't need the spotlight or the glory
 As long as I'm still able
 to tell my story

---

*They, Their, and Them Hymn

If I had a dime for every doubtful line I've heard
I'd be the richest inventor of words
They told me that I needed a real job
so as I spend my time working for strange Bobs
aiming to dispute the him, her, and them mob
I'll continue to nurture the belief in my soul
and formulate the greatest stories ever told
to refute the lies he and she concocted
tuck all of their negativity in my pocket
create my own memory locket
and years from now reveal what's inside
as proof that dreams can skyrocket

---

*Examine my floetic hooks
to find your way through my poetic nooks
I'm patiently waiting for a love crook
A Mr. Write who's willing to stop and look
while flipping through the pages
of my complicated life's book

---

*If words move mountains
 I guess I'm rearranging the hills
 Elevating altitudes and learning to comprehend
 my daily moods just by sharing how I feel
 You can't tell me dreams aren't real
 I'm staring mine in the grill, rolling without wheels
 Higher than any pill could ever get me
 I don't need counterfeit fifties or other thrifty
 materialistic gifts, see
 my pen is a nifty weapon that sets me free
 from all the stressin'
 when I think that life's a mess and
 I'm tired of givin' my best
 I'll still be pushing to pass God's test
 because he promised that someday I'd be blessed
 So even if I never get to touch the sky
 I'll keep the faith, continue to rise
 watch the clouds as they pass by
 and patiently wait for my moment to shine

---

*If I close my eyes I might miss out on a surprise
 So I'm wide awake dreaming
 while wearing my writer disguise
 Trying to save the world one word at a time

---

*Mo money
mo problems
but my success will dissolve them

---

*Got everything I could ever want or need
Except an H-U-S-B-A-N-D
Education, Career, Marriage, Kids was the plan
Didn't think I'd have to wait this long
for the perfect man
Guess I've been putting up a front
for the past 7 months
Single and supposed to be ready to mingle
I lied so I hide
Heartbreak number two has been a rough ride
but I find peace in my writing strides
Words will never hurt me
I'll always survive
At 25, I've accomplished more than most
Still I dream about that beautiful wedding toast
Love isn't an easy feat
As soon as me and Mr. Write meet
I know my heart will skip triple the beats
Third time's a charm
and I can't wait
to find comfort in his arms

---

*Thirsty for love
Tired of taking dry sips
Need a man who will look past
my nonexistent hips
and take skinny dips
into private invitations
of getting to know me
Slowly
Someone patient enough to break down these walls
and strong enough to catch me when I fall
That's all she wrote
but my words don't tell it all

---

*I was lost back then
Uncomfortable in
my own brown skin
and when I think of
where I could've been
How God washed away
every dirty sin
All that I can say is thank you

---

*When the words won't come out
I let them build up
and then I explode
Writer mode overload

---

*Deadlines, Dreams, Desires
If I reach any higher
my arms won't bend
But I'm almost at the end of the mission I started
Slightly departed for a month or two
and then I recapped, revamped and regrouped

*Is it wrong to attempt to do everything
you think you can?
I courageously hold up my right hand
every time I take the stand to recite my life plans:
Someday I'm going to write articles
for a newspaper beat,
find a full-time job that allows me
to utilize my degree,
publish a book or two,
maybe even three,
create my own online magazine,
and offer tutoring services
to kids who can't write or read.
My mission is to plant inspirational seeds
of good literary deeds with purified water...
in that order!
Now, what were you saying
about sticking to the norm?
Pssshh!
I refuse to conform.

*I wish I may
I wish I might
find the strength to write tonight
Constant dedication
but I lost my inspiration
When I saw that no one was interested
in reading my hymns
Don't they know I do this for them?
Capturing words in a daze
Hoping they would be amazed
by seeing what they were feeling
and just couldn't say

---

*I'm only a messenger
and messages aren't clear
when there's no support near
Where's my lifeline?
Can't continue my #WriterGrind
without loyal backing
The praise is there but sincerity is lacking
They don't want to see me rise
without expecting a prize
Even though I share my gift for free
How much more can I give?
I've already given them all of me

---

*I said goodbye but he looked at me
 with those eyes
 and that smile
 Silently begging me to stay awhile longer
 Today I'm a lot stronger
 because I knew it was time to let go
 Wasn't afraid to just say no
 Even though I wanted him
 to ask me to stay

*Dearly Beloved S.I.S.T.A.S
 Try being alone
 before sitting on another man's throne
 You keep petting that dog just because
 he barks at your bones
 Don't let him infect you with fleas
 Ignore that "baby please"
 when he's begging on his knees
 Dearly Beloved S.I.S.T.A.S
 You're just as fly on your own

*I found courage in a leap
 Closed my eyes, hoped that I would land
 on my feet... and here I stand
 Still, with a pen in my hand
 rocking to the beat. No drums, No keys
 Just an acapella rhyme scheme
 and a lifelong writing dream

*People keep telling me that
I can't complete this mission
"You're doing too much" they say
but dreams are a risky business
and I'm not afraid to take chances
So I refuse to listen
They be trippin'
Waiting for me to fall
victim
to their hater symptoms

---

*Love Me 365

3 words of bliss, the year split equals 6
Plus 5 minutes of writing this dedication list
to tell you how much I love to kiss your lips
Even though we've had some dips in the road
Our story will be the greatest ever told
Words bond us together
uWrite and iWrite and whether
or not we last forever
the memories of the time
we shared will always be better
than being alone

---

*I wake up with words on the tip of my tongue
and metaphors rocking to the tune of my lungs
I'll die fighting for writing

---

*My next will be my last
Can't move too fast
on this love expedition
My heart spoke and I listened
If you keep chasing after
what God doesn't want you to have
You're sure to miss it
Like a shooting star
my target isn't very far
If he aims for the moon
I know he'll find me soon

---

*All this corporate stuff is driving me nuts
They gon' make me cuss!
So ready to E-X-I-T
But I need M-O-N-E...
Y can't we all just survive
on our passion?
This isn't the type of life I imagined for myself
All I want to do is write and nothing else
Words bring me joy and wealth and love
I've had enough!
But in order to get to where I'm going
I can't give up
So I'll just fuss out loud in my head instead

---

*I remember how my heart broke
when I found those love notes
addressed to her
and
she
was not me
My sneak peeking
revealed that he was cheating
I didn't want to know
so
I
decided to let it go
and then he did it again
but I forgave him for his sins
Figured my heart would mend
until I started to cry one last tear
with every apology
he tried to squeeze in
He wasn't sorry
and I knew it
Silly of me to go through it
but I thought he was the one

*911 Plea

I want to fly, I mean touch the sky
Get so high that I can see the world through a bird's
eye view, and bid adieu to these American blues
Moments filled with sad news all around me
Trouble has found me and I can't escape.
Seems like it's too late to dream again.
They say the world is about to end
but I've got lots to accomplish before the last spin
I want to go home,
back to where my wings were necessary,
when I decided to live free and quite the contrary
to popular belief.
When emergencies arise can I just close my eyes
and breathe? I don't want to fall to my knees and
freeze at the sight of tragedies like these
I just want to fly... Just let me fly
please!

---

*My greatest victories are no longer a mystery
because I chose not to repeat the history
of those who came before me
they'll never adore me for not keeping it real
but my children's children
will have bigger shoes to fill

---

*Ain't no do-overs when it comes to life
 Wake up and get it right!
 I've only got one goal in sight
 when I lay myself down to sleep at night

*I'm not all work and no play
 but I won't let anything stand in my way
 Took me forever to be able to say
 That FIRST, I'll love me
 Finally learned the difference between
 what I want and what I need

*Y'all don't understand
 it took me years of blood, sweat, and tears
 to devise this plan
 don't ask me why I don't have a man
 I just haven't found anyone who's able to stand
 next to me with integrity
 So for now I'll rise alone
 and reach for success on my own
 couldn't say that months ago
 when I was settling for "all I know"
 but I decided to let it flow
 and let God run my show

*The Girl with the Tattoo

They say it's a sin to etch ink on your skin
Will God forgive me if I repent
and promise to never do it again?
It wasn't a deliberate moral diss
when I decided to get "iWrite"
engraved on my wrist
A symbol for the very reason I exist
Representation of purposeful days
for reasons other than an artsy display
Seeping through my veins with love
My heart pumps words instead of blood
When I'm down and out or feel like giving up
I just stop and stare at my permanent reminder buzz
and iWrite
iWrite
iWrite
until I've had enough

*Do you know how hard it is to be good all the time?
How desperately I wanted to commit a crime
just so people would stop pushing me up a mountain
I didn't want to climb
I wanted to be normal like everybody else
but I became an overachiever
and outshined myself
Fail once, they shame you
Fail twice, they blame you
Fail three times, people no longer claim you
Nobody's perfect
but I felt like I had to be
because no one would ever accept failure from me
Average wasn't enough
so I forced myself to accomplish
the impossible stuff
and then I got comfortable with the thought
of never giving up
Learned to love being in the spotlight
with everyone showering me with praise
transitioned into my "I believe I can fly" phase
Now, I see a new me every time I look in the mirror
Vowed that someday I would be known as
more than just Tomboy Tera

*I had a premonition
with doubt clouding my vision
and fear climbing its way in
without permission
how could I believe that my dreams
would come to fruition?
I was in a tough position
but I knew that God would listen
I told Him my plan
and asked Him to guide me along the way
His response was "Be still"
That's all He had to say
So I waited
Waited 14 long years for this day
I'll share my vision with the world
and continue to pray
Dreams will eventually become reality,
Even after what seems like
a forever delay

---

*I love metaphors
and similes
Haikus
and epiphanies
The rhythms
and the symphonies
of words
I'm a writer nerd

---

*I have a dream
That one day I'll see my books
on shelves around the world,
That I'll be able to share my stories
with lots of boys and girls
That I'll write unforgettable scenes
and characters that never die
That I'll make people laugh
and also make them cry
I had a dream
Age 25, independent and free
Age 30, a bestselling author I will be
I have a dream
I'll inspire others to explore their passion
in any shape, form, or fashion
To follow the stars to the sky's limit
To explore and exhibit
To travel and visit that place within
To live it and go get it
To conquer and win
I have a dream
What's yours?

LRW QUOTES

Distractions deter dreams.

Life is like a rollercoaster. It goes round and round, up and down... and then the ride is over.

Take your best shot(s) at life. Even if you keep throwing up bricks, the swish will come eventually.

The choices you make will determine the future you'll face.

We must sacrifice for the sake of fulfillment. Don't let fear shatter your desires.

Betterment is not attainable if one refuses to adjust hindering mannerisms.

When you are doing what you love, you will never feel like you are working too hard to get too little. No salary is greater than satisfaction.

True leaders leave footsteps for admirers to follow... but the admirer must create his or her own milestone in order to take the lead.

The cleansing process brings peace of mind. You have to take the bandage off of the wound in order for it to heal.

My future is bright... in living color.

A job is just a passionless time filler that one chooses to endure until the opportunity comes for them to passionately pursue their dream.

Those who are unable to correct their selfish nature forfeit the privilege to love properly.

"I love you" is a three word phrase that everyone finds pleasure in hearing. Saying "I wrote that" is equivalent to that pleasure for me.

Proud moments outlast happy ones.

When dreams become nightmares, hope will save the day.

Blessings are contagious.

The timing of an apology will sometimes be too little too late for forgiveness.

No matter how complicated life gets, music will always make sense.

The surety in trying outlasts the regret in giving up.

You don't know what you want until you know what you don't want. What you want should be worth wanting and when it isn't worth wanting anymore that's when you should let it go.

Enough is enough will never be enough as enough is enough right now.

Time is wasted when two people aren't looking at the same clock.

Faith is believing while knowing the difference between impossible and realistic.

Success is like a train. Everyone wants to jump on board after you've reached your final destination.

Complacency is like a stale bag of chips. If you sit around and wait for things to happen, you will eventually begin to lose your crunch.

What's a mistake if you don't learn from it? What's a profit if you don't earn from it? What's love if you don't burn from it?

There can be no trust without truth.

Being passively dormant produces no reward. Success is birthed through ambitious growth, not lackadaisical hope.

To truly focus, one must completely surrender all distracting sources.

My byline is my my line.

Love is a battlefield of blame, but war doesn't always have to end in pain.

Conversation versus communication proposes a new rule of understanding... Reading between the lines of what is implied while recognizing the difference between the truth and a lie.

Forgive and forget... or live and regret.

Communication is the key to everything, in life and in love. Silence has never unlocked any doors.

In a writer's world, time is the only villain.

What ifs don't matter in the presence of certainty.

Unread words are unrevealed secrets.

I don't want to be famous... I just want to be remembered.

Regrets can't be recovered.

What's the secret to success? Work hard... Work harder!

The difference between a career and a job can be calculated by measuring the balance of smiling vs. complaining.

An epiphany is the greatest form of discovery.

Every form of pain is a new writing gain.

Dreaming with my eyes wide open... every blink leads me closer to reality.

Some characters in your life are only meant to be present during one scene. It's up to you to decide if you want to spend unnecessary time rereading the first page or move on to the excitement within the next chapter.

Avoidance is the primary cause of misunderstandings and assumptions... Communicate to alleviate confused states of speculation.

I grew up in the hood and graduated to good... Now I'm on my way to great.

The word "can't" is a profane expression that hinders the hope for success. Don't let pessimistic tendencies ruin your possibilities. (C)ease (A)ll (N)egativity (T)oday!

The only thing that comes to a sleeper is a dream. I like the way mine looks when I'm wide awake.

The difference between being the boss of yourself and being bossed by someone else is evidently clear... The latter prevents you from being able to control your own destiny.

Sometimes being friends is more beneficial than being lovers. Two individuals who are mature enough to appreciate and understand the differences between both connections will be able to develop a long-lasting relationship that is not bound by obligation or guilt.

It's better to give than receive... even more better to have faith and believe.

To be physically absent from reality and effectively present with words is the ultimate writer victory.

If everyone had someone to give them a much needed motivational kick, we'd all be walking on sunshine.

Big mistakes are sometimes hard to forgive. Best mistakes are always worth it to live.

God will do what He said He will do… but only if you do what He says.

To discipline without purposeful intention is to spoil without positive gain.

Sorries are the most important element of forgiveness.

True motivation is often discovered after acknowledging someone else's success.

Freedom reveals itself at the end of every decision that is not like you.

You know nothing until you've learned something.

Mix a little courage with a lot of Faith and trust God to add the remaining ingredients.

Naysayers are often the primary inspiration for accomplishing life goals.

Dreams become reality when sacrifices become obligations.

When your stories become your life, your life becomes your stories.

Turn that 'I think I can' into an 'I believe I can' and Just Do It.

Wasted time is an irretrievable treasure that interrupts life pleasures.

Sometimes listening is more worthwhile than talking, especially when the person who is doing the talking is often misunderstood.

Forgiveness is to love as water is to roses, necessary for growth and development.

Consequences should inspire change. Better is best!

Love is blind, but it isn't invisible.

You can't completely enjoy success if you continue to hold on to things and people that hinder your happiness... Especially those who don't want to be held… L.I.G (Let It Go)!

Language marks... and I'm puncturing the world with my literary tattoos.

When life gives you lemons, make lemonade... when it gives you apples, make apple juice... when it gives you oranges, make 'Sunny D' and 'shine' your 'light' on the world.

When you recognize the gift(s) that God intentionally blessed you with, it is your duty to utilize them in every way possible.

If you're living without giving, your talents are null and void.

#WriterGrind

www.ingramcontent.com/pod-product-compliance
Lightning Source LLC
Chambersburg PA
CBHW072022040426
42447CB00009B/1697